Flowers and Insects

Some Birds and a Pair of Spiders

for Frieda and Lucretia

Flowers and Insects

Some Birds and a Pair of Spiders

TED HUGHES

**With drawings by
LEONARD BASKIN**

faber and faber
LONDON · BOSTON

First published in 1986
by Faber and Faber Limited
3 Queen Square London WC1N 3AU

Designed and produced for the publishers
by Pilot Productions Limited
59 Charlotte Street London W1P 1LA

'An Almost Thornless Crown' was published in *The Times* as part of
'A Birthday Pageant for Her Majesty Queen Elizabeth's Sixtieth
Birthday'; 'A Violet At Lough Aughrisburg' and 'Where I Sit Writing
My Letter' were originally published in *The Listener*; 'Narcissi' first
appeared in *The Observer*, and 'Daffodils' and 'Nightjar' in *The London
Review of Books*; 'Two Tortoiseshell Butterflies', 'Sunstruck Foxglove'
and 'In The Likeness Of A Grass-hopper' were first published in
London Magazine, 'Big Poppy' in *New Republic*, and 'Saint's Island' in
Grand Street; both 'Tern' and 'Eclipse' appeared in privately printed
limited editions by Scolar and The Sceptre Press respectively.

Hughes, Ted
  Flowers and Insects
  I. Title
  821'.914   PR6058.U37

  ISBN 0-571-13317-7

Typeset by Rowland Phototypesetting (London) Ltd
Colour origination by RCS Graphics Leeds LS28 5LY
Printed by Mandarin Offset Marketing (H.K.) Ltd

FIRST EDITION

CONTENTS

NARCISSI

The Narcissi shiver their stars
In the green-gold wind of evening sunglare.
Their happiness is weightless.
Their merriment is ghostly.

Tonight, too, will be precarious stars
On the Moon's hill
And an April frost.

The Narcissi are untouchable
In a rustling, silent film
Of speeded-up dancing
And laughing children
From the 1918 Armistice.

Their tiny faces are pinched
Under big, loose bows of pale ribbon.

But this is happiness now
To be grown up—
                    skinny, modish girls,
Hair blown back, thin lips parted, pressing
Into a cold sunglare, cheekbones flared
And delicate as lit ice.

They will never be hurt.

(Even among the mourners,
Harrowed with solemnity, and chilled,
They will be safe—

Bulbs in earth
Under the shock of the wreath.)

                    Starry wreath.

Ghost-lights in the orchard.

A VIOLET AT LOUGH AUGHRISBURG

The tide-swell grinds crystal, under cliffs.

Against the opened furnace of the West—
A branch of apple-blossom.

A bullock of sooted bronze
Cools on an emerald
That is crumbling to granite embers.

Milk and blood are frail
In the shivering wind off the sea.

    Only a purple flower—this amulet
    (Once Prospero's)—holds it all, a moment,
    In a rinsed globe of light.

BRAMBLES

The whole air, the whole day
Swirls with the calls of jackdaws. The baby jackdaw
Generation is being initiated
Into jackdawdom—that complicated
Court-world of etiquette

And precedence, jingoism and law.
Nearly a prison world—with bars
Of cries and signals. The jailors
Are all the other jackdaws. Tearing a track
Through the intertangled briars

I thought again: do they feel this?
Briars are such a success, their defences
So craftsmanlike,
Their reachings so deliberate, are they awake?
Surely some nimbus of pain and pleasure

Sits on their naked coronet,
Their sexual offer. Surely they aren't just numb,
A blind groping. Yet why not?
Aren't my blood-cells the same?
What do even brain-cells fear or feel

Of the scalpel, or the accident?
They too crown a plant
Of peculiar numbness. And the jackdaws
Work darkly to be jackdaws
As if they were seeds in the earth.

The whole claque is a benighted religion
Around the godlike syntax and vocabulary
Of a mute cell, that does not know who we are
Or even that we are here,
Unforthcoming as any bramble-flower.

DAFFODILS

I'd bought a patch of wild ground.
In March it surprised me. Suddenly I saw what I
                                                owned.
A cauldron of daffodils, boiling gently.

A gilding of the Deeds—treasure trove!
Daffodils just came. And kept coming—

"Blown foam," I wrote, "Vessels of light!"
They raced under every gust
On the earth-surge. "Their six-bladed screws
Churning the greeny-yellows
Out of the hard, over-wintered Chlorophyl."

I was still a nomad.
My life was still a raid. The earth was booty.
I knew I'd live forever. I had not learned
What a fleeting glance of the everlasting
Daffodils are. Did not recognise
The nuptial flight of the rarest ephemera—
My own days!
Hardly more body than a hallucination!
A dream of gifts—opening their rustlings for me!

I thought they were a windfall. I picked them. I sold
                                                them.

Behind the rainy curtains of that dark April
I became intimate
With the soft shrieks
Of their jostled stems—
The wet shocks shaken
Of their girlish dance-frocks—
Fresh-opened Dragonflies, wet and flimsy.

To each scared, bright glance
I brought a defter cruelty. So many times
Slid my fingers down her slenderness,

Felt for the source, her chilly fount,
The watery flicker she peered from,
And nipped her off close to the bulb.

I piled their frailty lights on a carpenter's bench,
Distributed leaves among the dozens
(Buckling blade-leaves, limber, groping for air,
                                        zinc-silvered)
Propped their raw butts in bucket water
(Their oval, meaty butts)
And sold them, sevenpence a bunch. The whole lot
                                        went.

Yet they stayed. That night, on my pillow,
My brain was a chandelier of daffodils!

Wings pouring light, faces bowed,
Dressed for Heaven,
The souls of all those daffodils, as I killed them,
Had gone to ground inside me—there they were
                                        packed.

I could see right into their flame-stillness
Like seeing right into the eye-pupil
Of a person fast asleep, as if I'd lifted the eyelid—

I could study
That scarf of papery crinkle, fawn and perfunctory, at
                                        their throats,
And the tissue of their lips. I learned
That what had looked like a taffeta knot, undone
And re-tied looser, crumpled,
Was actually membrane of solid light.

And that their metals were odourless,
More a deep grave stoniness, a cleanness of stone,
As if ice had a breath—

They began to alarm me. Were these
My free girls, my Saturnalian nunnery

With their bloomers of scrambled egg-yolk, their
flounces,
Their core so alive and kicking, their bare shoulders
in frills,
That set the cold stars shaking
Loose and wetly
Inside walking, darkly-coated people?

I tried to picture them out there—in the garden—

These rigid, gold archangels somehow
Drank up my attempt.
They became awful,
Like the idea of atoms. Or like the idea
Of white-frosted galaxies, floating apart.

As I sank deeper, each towered heavier,
Cathedral interior lit,
Empty or all-seeing angel stare
Leaning through me—

     It was Resurrection!
The trumpet!
The earth-weight of nightmare!
       I wrenched free.
I flitted
With my world, my garden, my unlikely
Baby-cries leached from the thaw—
       my shiverers
In the draughty wings of the year—

TWO TORTOISESHELL BUTTERFLIES

Mid-May—after May frosts that killed the Camellias,
After May snow. After a winter
Worst in human memory, a freeze
Killing the hundred year old Bay Tree,
And the ten year old Bay Tree—suddenly
A warm limpness. A blue heaven just veiled
With the sweatings of earth
And with the sweatings-out of winter
Feverish under the piled
Maywear of the lawn.
                              Now two
Tortoiseshell butterflies, finding themselves alive,
She drunk with the earth-sweat, and he
Drunk with her, float in eddies
Over the Daisies' quilt. She prefers Dandelions,
Settling to nod her long spring tongue down
Into the nestling pleats, into the flower's
Thick-folded throat, her wings high-folded.

He settling behind her, among plain glistenings
Of the new grass, edging and twitching
To nearly touch—pulsing and convulsing
Wings wide open to tight-closed to flat open
Quivering to keep her so near, almost reaching
To stroke her abdomen with his antennae—
Then she's up and away, and he startlingly
Swallowlike overtaking, crowding her, heading her
Off any escape. She turns that
To her purpose, and veers down
Onto another Dandelion, attaching
Her weightless yacht to its crest.
Wobbles to stronger hold, to deeper, sweeter
Penetration, her wings tight shut above her,
A sealed book, absorbed in itself.
She ignores him
Where he edges to left and to right, flitting
His wings open, titillating her fur
With his perfumed draughts, spasming his patterns,
His tropical, pheasant appeals of folk-art,
Venturing closer, grass-blade by grass-blade,
Trembling with inhibition, nearly touching—
And again she's away, dithering blackly . He swoops

20

On an elastic to settle accurately
Under her tail again as she clamps to
This time a Daisy. She's been chosen,
Courtship has claimed her. And he's been
                                        conscripted
To what's required
Of the splitting bud, of the talented robin
That performs piercings
Out of the still-bare ash,
The whole air just like him, just breathing
Over the still-turned-inward earth, the first
Caresses of the wedding coming, the earth
Opening its petals, the whole sky
Opening a flower
Of unfathomably-patterned pollen.

CYCLAMENS IN A BOWL

A pink one. A white one. Each
A butterfly—caught by an uptwisting
Slender snake and held. Without hurt.
Without fear.

Now, it seems, a serpent of plants
Rearing and angling, gently writhing
Has opened a butterfly face.

The five petals elated—
A still of tensile flight!

The great, wide-awake ears
Of the most lady-like of gazelles
A gerenuk, in mid-leap,
Over the ambush of clumsy body-leaves.

The flower escapes

The leaves and stems toil in sturdy pursuit,
Debating their manoeuvres with each other,
Arranging their groupings in a workaday world.

The flower floats off into trance
Unattached
At the open window—

Deepening, with skirts up over its head,
Into the breathless
Brightenings that embrace it—

(The lambent, electric shock-waves
Of our simply, quietly gazing at it)

Cool flame-tongue, spectre flower of the lungs!
Wing-beat that nests in the pelvis!
Soul-bird of the bowels!
The heart's very throb
As a winged Hallelujah!

Uplifted, upheld
Letting the God-light glow through—

While the solid leaves, physiques of substance,
Forest-dark, patched pale with experience,
Burdened with passionate, lush, vulnerable veins,
Open their palms to the air, simple and good,

Under those rearing, plunging fillies of spirit!

SAINT'S ISLAND
for Barrie Cooke

This is a day for small marvels.
The Mayflies are leaving their Mother.

Seven horse-power, our bows batter
The ridgy Lough.
Weird womb. Beneath us
It gestates a monster—

Monstrous, but tiny. When it appears
We'll call it The Green Drake.
At the moment, down there in the mud,
It's something else—
The dream of an alchemist,

The nightmare
Of the sunk pebble
That feels the claws grip lightly.

But today—it wants to be born.
It's had enough of the mud. At a brainwave,
Overpowered by it does not know what
(What is it doing on earth, anyway?)
It kicks off from its burrow.
                                        It rises
Fuelled by the manias of space
And inspiration
That coil round the sun's mask.

It rises, as if it fell,
Towards that magnet core, where blindness glances,
The sun's water-image
Shivered by our shock-wave, as we bounce past.

The Mayflies are leaving their Mother.

I glimpse one labouring—a close-up
In the brow of a wave.

I glimpse the midget sneeze—
A dream bursts its bubble.
As much machinery
As the upspurge of a big oak.
(One time I found one had failed.
It wallowed in the oil of light.
I saw through my lens a tiny leech
Corkscrewed into its head.)
Luckier, in millions,
A catkin-green, dragonish torso
Hauls from its sleeping bag—
A yacht has a blown, stubborn moment—
Falters, lifts from the Lough's melt—

The Mayflies are leaving their Mother.

And there they go. The Lough's words to the world.
This is what it thinks.
This is what it aspires to, finally.
This is the closest it comes
To consciousness, and the flight into light—

Into life?

All morning, leaving their Mother, the Mayflies
Spinning on their weak centres,
Poetic electrons
With their vision of the sun's skirts
(An idea faceted like a fly's eye,
A rose-window in blood-cells,
A Holy Grail of neurons)
Blow and dither downwind

Toward the Island,
Toward the grey crumble of Monastery.

They crowd in under the boughs,
Keels under every leaf,
Dangle on claws, cluster their ripenings,
Letting the sun touch them through Chlorophyl,

27

Spooky fruit

Spooky because this isn't their world
Their world is over.
Their feastings are complete. Their jaws are tied up.
This is their underworld,
Their beach-head in death, because they are already
souls—

So many
They gauze and web the Maybush bloom and leaf
As they digest their shock,
The vision.
It nourishes them,
It consumes them.
It peels off the last drudgery
Of the Lough

And they are creeping out of their lives.
None resist or defer it,

29

Or settle for terms, or evade it.
Already
They have dressed themselves in Mayfly, a lace of
                                        blackish crystals

(As if our lives were lichenous rock
Or a sleep of roots. Or a tin of sardines,
An apple, a watch, a thermos.)

Everywhere under the leaves
You see their mummy moulds,
The refuse of their earthliness, clinging empty,
The blood-chart in their wings still perfect,
Still waiting (already seeming dusty),

But they've gone up into sunlight, a wet shimmer

In their smudgy veils,
Sooty fairies.

We watch them through binocs. On and off
All day till evening
They are dancing above the trees, rising and falling
To woodwind airs, clouded or sunny,
To bowings
Of thermometer and barometer,
Over and over, a reel unending and Irish—

What time will they come out? Will they come out?

No hurry,
The long-bellied females, pith-naked,
Tender two inch snippets of live nerve-cord
Tipped with the three black fork hairs even longer,
And the males darker, smaller—
They are rediscovering each other.
Familiars of the ten billion years

They jig in a spin, in a column. They are tossed and
                                        are tossed—

Their happiness is to prolong this. To prolong it
Till the moment opens—and it happens—
And an escaping climax of the music
Lifts them over the top—

And they are coming out!

But now like Dervishes, truly they are like those,
Touched by God,
Drunk with God, they hurl themselves into God—

They have caught the moment,
Their dancing has found that fault in time
To break through—to break out—
Into beyond—
They are casting themselves away,
They abandon themselves, they soar out of
                                        themselves,
They fall through themselves—

Where can they go?

Space can't hold them. The blue air is snowing.

All round us
Trickling giddily down, they try to pirouette.

The wind carries them out.

Under the outer waves of the Lough
The big trout wait.
Under the Island lee, anchored in the mirror,
Between light and dark, on the skin of shivers,
We wait.
          (What are we doing on earth?)

All round us
Fanatics faint and wreck shuddering, gently,
Onto the face of evening.

WHERE I SIT WRITING MY LETTER

Suddenly hooligan baby starlings
Rain all round me squealing,
Shouting how it's tremendous and everybody
Has to join in and they're off this minute!

Probably the weird aniseed corpse-odour
Of the hawthorn flower's disturbed them,
As it disturbs me. Now they all rise
Flutter-floating, oddly eddying,

Squalling their dry gargles. Then, mad, they
Hurl off, on a new wrench of excitement,
Leaving me out.
                I pluck apple-blossom,
Cool, blood-lipped, wet open.

And I'm just quieting thoughts towards my letter
When they all come storming back,
Giddy with hoarse hissings and snarls
And clot the top of an ash sapling—

Sizzling bodies, snaky black necks craning
For a fresh thrill—Where next? Where now?
                Where?—they're off
All rushing after it
Leaving me fevered, and addled.

They can't believe their wings.

Snow-bright clouds boil up.

TERN
                for Norman Nicholson

The breaker humps its green glass.
You see the sunrise through it, the wrack dark in it,
And over it—the bird of sickles
Swimming in the wind, with oiled spasm.

That is the tern. A blood-tipped harpoon
Hollow-ground in the roller-dazzle,
Honed in the wind-flash, polished
By his own expertise—

Now finished and in use.
The wings—remote-controlled
By the eyes
In his submarine swift shadow

Feint and tilt in their steel.
Suddenly a triggered magnet
Connects him downward, through a thin shatter,
To a sand-eel. He hoists out, with a twinkling,

Through some other wave-window.
His eye is a gimlet.
Deep in the churned grain of the roller
His brain is a gimlet. He hangs,

A blown tatter, a precarious word
In the mouth of ocean pronouncements.
His meaning has no margin. He shudders
To the tips of his tail-tines.

Momentarily, his lit scrap is a shriek.

SKETCH OF A GODDESS

We have one Iris. A Halberd
Of floral complications. Two blooms are full,
Floppily opened, or undone rather.
                                        Royal
Seraglio twin sisters, contending
For the Sultan's eye. Even here
One is superior.
Rivalry has devastated
Everything about them except
The womb's temptation and offer.

That one's past it. But this one's in her prime.
She utters herself
Utterly into appeal. A surrender
Of torn mucous membranes, veined and purpled,
A translucence of internal organs
In a frisson,
Torn open,
The core debauched,
All loosely dangling helplessness
And enfolding claspers—

Delicately holding herself
As if every edge were cringing round a nerve.

Actually
She's lolling her tongue right out,
Her uvula arched,
Her uterus everted—

An overpowered bee buries its face
In the very beard of her ovaries.

It deafens itself
In a dreadful belly-cry—just out of human hearing.

THE HONEY BEE

The Honey Bee
Brilliant as Einstein's idea
Can't be taught a thing.
Like the sun, she's on course forever.

As if nothing else at all existed
Except her flowers.
No mountains, no cows, no beaches, no shops.
Only the rainbow waves of her flowers

A tremor in emptiness

A flying carpet of flowers

                              —a pattern
Coming and going—very loosely woven—
Out of which she works her solutions.

Furry goblin midgets
(The beekeeper's thoughts) clamber stickily
Over the sun's face—gloves of shadow.

But the Honey Bee
Cannot imagine him, in her brilliance,

Though he's a stowaway on her carpet of
                                        colour-waves
And drinks her sums.

IN THE LIKENESS OF A GRASS-HOPPER

A trap
Waits on the field path.

A wicker contraption, with working parts,
Its spring tensed and set.

So flimsily made, out of grass
(Out of the stems, the joints, the raspy-dry flags).

Baited with a fur-soft caterpillar,
A belly of amorous life, pulsing signals.

Along comes a love-sick, perfume-footed
Music of the wild earth.

The trap, touched by a breath,
Jars into action, its parts blur –

And music cries out.

A sinewy violin
Has caught its violinist.

Cloud-fingered summer, the beautiful trapper,
Picks up the singing cage

And takes out the Song, adds it to the Songs
With which she robes herself, which are her wealth,

Sets her trap again, a yard further on.

SUNSTRUCK FOXGLOVE

As you bend to touch
The gypsy girl
Who waits for you in the hedge
Her loose dress falls open.

Midsummer ditch-sickness!

Flushed, freckled with earth-fever,
Swollen lips parted, her eyes closing,
A lolling armful, and so young! Hot

Among the insane spiders.
You glimpse the reptile under-speckle
Of her sunburned breasts
And your head swims. You close your eyes.

Can the foxes talk? Your head throbs.
Remember the bird's tolling echo,
The dripping fern-roots, and the butterfly touches
That woke you.

Remember your mother's
Long, dark dugs.

Her silky body a soft oven
For loaves of pollen.

ECLIPSE

For half an hour, through a magnifying glass,
I've watched the spiders making love undisturbed,
Ignorant of the voyeur, horribly happy.

First in the lower left-hand corner of the window
I saw an average spider stirring. There
In a midden of carcases, the shambles
Of insects dried in their colours,
A trophy den of uniforms, reds, greens,
Yellow-striped and detached wing-frails, last year's
Leavings, parched a winter, scentless—heads,
Bodices, corsets, leg-shells, a crumble of shards
In a museum of dust and neglect, there
In the crevice, concealed by corpses in their old
                                           wrappings,
A spider has come to live. She has spun
An untidy nearly invisible
Floss of strands, a few aimless angles
Camouflaged as the grey dirt of the rain-stains
On the glass. I saw her moving. Then a smaller,
Just as ginger, similar all over,
Only smaller. He had suddenly appeared.

Upside down, she was doing a gentle
Sinister dance. All legs clinging
Except for those leading two, which tapped on the
                                           web,
Trembling it, I thought, like a fly, to attract
The immobile, upside-down male, near the frame,
Only an inch from her. He moved away,
Turning ready to flee, I guessed. Maybe
Fearful of her intentions and appetites:
Doubting. But her power, focussing,
Making no error after the millions of years
Perfecting this art, turned him round
At a distance of two inches, and hung him
Upside down, head under, belly towards her.
Motionless, except for a faint

And just-detectable throb of his hair-leg tips.
She came closer, upside down, gently,
And enmeshed his forelegs in hers.

So, I imagined, here is the famous murder.
I got closer to watch. Something
Difficult to understand, difficult
To properly observe was going on.
Her two hands seemed swollen, like tiny crab-claws.
Those two nippers she folds up under nose
To bring things to her pincers, they were moving,
Glistening. He convulsed now and again.
Her abdomen pod twitched—spasmed slightly
Little mean ecstasies. Was she pulling him to pieces?
Something much more delicate, a much more
Delicate agreement was in process.
Under his abdomen he had a nozzle—
Presumably his lumpy little cock,
Just as ginger as the rest of him, a teat,
An infinitesimal nipple. Probably
Under a microscope it is tooled and designed
Like some micro-device in a space rocket.
To me it looked crude and simple. Far from simple,
Though, were her palps, her boxing-glove nippers—
They were like the mechanical hands
That manipulate radio-active matter
On the other side of safe screen glass.
But hideously dexterous. She reached out one,
I cannot imagine how she saw to do it,
And brought monkey-fingers from under her
                                        crab-nippers
And grasped his nipple cock. As soon as she had it
A bubble of glisteny clear glue
Ballooned up from her nipper, the size of her head,
Then shrank back, and as it shrank back
She wrenched her grip off his cock
As if it had locked there, and doubled her fistful
Of shining wet to her jaw-pincers
And rubbed her mouth and underskin with it,
Six, seven stiff rubs, while her abdomen twitched,
Her tail-tip flirted, and he hung passive.
Then out came her other clutcher, on its elbow,
And grabbed his bud, and the gloy-thick bubble
Swelled above her claws, a red spur flicked

48

Inside it, and he jerked in his ropes.
Then the bubble shrank and she twisted it off
And brought it back to stuff her face-place
With whatever it was. Very still,
Except for those stealths and those twitchings
They hung upside down, face to face,
Holding forelegs. It was still obscure
Just what was going on. It went on.
Half an hour. Finally she backed off.
He hung like a dead spider, just as he'd hung
All the time she'd dealt with him.

I thought it must be over. So now, I thought,
I see the murder. I could imagine now
If he stirred she'd think he was a fly,
And she'd be feeling ravenous. And so far
She'd shown small excitement about him
With all that concentration on his attachment,
As if he upside down were just the table
Holding the delicacy. She moved off.
Aimlessly awhile she moved round,
Till I realised she was concentrating
On a V of dusty white, a delta
Of floss that seemed just fuzz. Then I could see
How she danced her belly low in the V.
I saw her fitting, with accurate whisker-fine feet,
Blobs of glue to the fibres, and sticking others
To thicken and deepen the V, and knot its juncture.
Then she danced in place, belly down, on this—
Suddenly got up and hung herself
Over the V. Sitting in the cup of the V
Was a tiny blob of new whiteness.
A first egg? Already? Then very carefully
She dabbed at the blob, and worked more woolly
                                                              fibres
Into the V, to either side of it,
Diminishing it as she dabbed. I could see
I was watching mighty nature
In a purposeful mood, but not what she worked at.
Soon, the little shapeless dot of white
Was a dreg of speck, and she left it. She returned
Towards her male, who hung still in position.
She paused and laboriously cleaned her hands,
Wringing them in her pincers. And suddenly
With a swift, miraculously-accurate snatch
Took something from her mouth, and dumped it
On an outermost cross-strand of web—
A tiny scrap of white—refuse, I thought,
From their lovemaking. So I stopped watching.
Ten minutes later they were at it again.
Now they have vanished. I have scrutinised
The whole rubbish tip of carcases

And the window-frame crannies beneath it.
They are hidden. Is she devouring him now?
Or are there still some days of bliss to come
Before he joins her antiques. They are hidden
Probably together in the fusty dark,
Holding forearms, listening to the rain, rejoicing
As the sun's edge, behind the clouds,
Comes clear of our shadow.

BIG POPPY

Hot-eyed Mafia Queen!
At the trim garden's edge

She sways towards August.
A Bumble Bee
Clambers into her drunken, fractured goblet—

Up the royal carpet of a down-hung,
Shrivel-edged, unhinged petal, her first-about-to-fall.
He's in there as she sways. He utters thin

Sizzling bleats of difficult enjoyment.
Her carnival paper skirts, luminous near-orange,
Embrace him helplessly.

Already her dark pod is cooking its drug.
Every breath imperils her. Her crucible
Is falling apart with its own fierceness.

A fly, cool, rests on the flame-fringe.

Soon she'll throw off her skirts
Withering into vestal afterlife,

Bleeding inwardly
Her maternal nectars into her own
Coffin—(cradle of her offspring).

Then we shall say:
"She wore herself in her hair, in her day,
And we could see nothing but her huge flop of petal,

Her big, lewd, bold eye, in its sooty lashes,

And that stripped, athletic leg, hairy,
In a fling of abandon—"

NIGHTJAR

The tree creeps on its knees.
The dead branch aims, in the last light.
The cat-bird is telescopic.

The sun's escape
Shudders, shot
By wings of ashes.

The moon falls, with all its moths,
Into a bird's face.

Stars spark
From the rasp of its cry.

Till the moon-eater, cooling,
Yawns dawn
And sleeps bark.

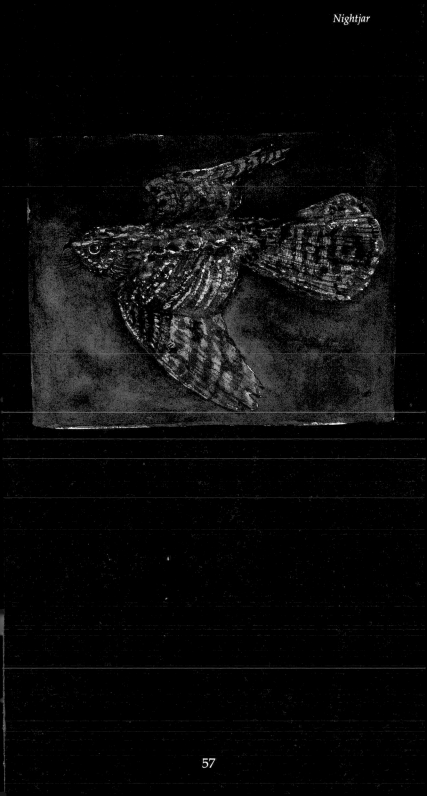

AN ALMOST THORNLESS CROWN
Titania Choreographs a Ballet, Using Her Attendants

Let the first be a Snowdrop, her neck bowed
Watching her modesty—
Her spermy, fattening gland
Cold under the ground.
                      Let her link an arm
With a Foxglove, raggily dressed,
Long-bodied, a rough blood-rope
Of dark nipples and full cup.
                      So she links
With a Daffodil—one
Whose chill, scrubbed face, and cold throat
Looks utterly true and pure,
The hail on her nape, her bare feet in mire.

And let her twine her arm around one a Rose
Who just now woke
And wakes wider, seems
To stretch awake, to peel back
Bedclothes, to throw off nightdress—to step
Into the shower, almost to sing
Flush with morning light—but cannot
Wake below the neck, or let sunbeams
Into the sleeping earth (who makes this
Effort in its dream, stirring a little).

Let her be linked
With somebody slender and tall, autumnal Balsam,
The full pitcher trembling, at evening—
Humid, soul-drinking insect,
Like a child bride of Nepal
In her pinkish-purple Sari, slightly too big for her,
Over-painted by temple harlots.

Weave in among
More Daffodils—find some nervy daughters,
Sober sisters, bonnets stiffly bowed
Watching the gravestones,

Equinox
Flint-raw and steely in their glances,
Who touch at themselves with cold fingers
And think upright thoughts.

(Though sometimes they wake in a scare
Laughing, hearing the mad can-can music,
And it comes over them
To dash off, wilder every minute,
Bare-legged in their tatters,
Away alongside scruffy rivers—

But they recover, they shake their heads, they bow,
Become the silent bells of the gust
That frightens the big tree.)
                                        Now here and there
A Pansy, little pug-face,
Baby Panda—
An intricate, masterly Japanese brush
Dabbed her identity signature—
                                        and twine in
                                            among all these
Hot and tipsy Honeysuckles,
Their gawky grace, their dark burgundy flushes
Already silked a little
As each one dips her neck through our exclamations,
And opens a gentle hydra
To sip human dreams,
Lips parted, a filament of salmon
Between the tongue and the teeth, a child's eye in a
                                        woman's body,
This little rhubarb dragon,
This viper in the leaves
Bites a numbness, in an anaesthetic perfume,
Her damage done so kindly
Her clutch of heart-shock, splitting trumpets
Softens into a scrollwork of eyelashes.

Now weave in the lofty Arum Lily,
Who hunches her fleshless scapulae,

And recites in silence from *Imitatio Christi*
With a demented grin.
Her sweat congeals to pearl
In a seminary of the profane,
Fallen stars her sole nutriment.

Link her with one more Rose
Whose dumb appeal cannot be decoded.
Not a lyrical cry, like the anguished Lily,
But a muffled thunder of perturbation—
Wide open, but her secret averted,
Mountain behind mountain, dawn beyond dawn.

And now a Cyclamen—her breathless dance
A ballerina, soaring
Over her astounded audience.

And now the heavy part, a tumbling peal of
                                   rhododendrons,
The knickerbocker lobes, the excess crumple of lips
Shadowed with bloodier darkness,
A cry from deep in the plant, hurting the throat and
                            the mouth helpless open,
A rejoicing, announcing burden of cry,
An offering cry, and the mouth left open—
Like the body offering of a beast, that bewilders the
                            eyes of the beast,
The love-offering of eyes, that bewilders the
                                 eyelids—
A faint stipple of freckles darkening the fine tissue.

Link all into a circle
With more Snowdrops.   Snowdrops half under
                                   snow
Waiting to be freed,
As 19th Century vicarage maidens
Erect, bare-shouldered, bowed, waiting for grace
At a tea-party—
Their faces are so childish!
A congregation of bells,

Tiny domes
Of serious worship—
                          all Cordelias.
Or else all green-veined Gonerils
Under the empty frenzy of hoar-frost.

Or a little court, all Queens,
Listening for the Moon.